The Business Owner's Savings Bible

27 Savings Secrets Your Business Can't Survive Without

Copyright © 2016 by Ed Klaameyer

Author Email: SavingsBiz.Ed@gmail.com

For permission write to: Global Profit Resources, llc.

Copyright & Trademarks

4821 Everhart Drive

Land O Lakes, FL 34639

Email: info@globalprofitresources.com

To book the author to speak at your event, business meeting or symposium, contact us at info@globalprofitresources.com, 813-318-1012.

ISBN: 978-0-9975120-0-7

Published by SAVVY Publisher

Printed in the United States of America.

THE BUSINESS OWNER'S SAVINGS BIBLE

27 Savings Secrets
Your Business
Can't Survive Without

Ed Klaameyer

DEDICATION

I dedicate this book to Jan, my wife, whose belief in me as a husband, father and businessman has been unwavering since we first met. Over these many years, she has continued to encourage me, support me, love me and pray for me. I will be forever grateful as she has helped me uncover and recognize my true potential.

FOREWARD

If you are going into business for the first time, you will need to develop an overall plan or strategy. If you are a business owner or manager, you need to follow a business plan to ensure sustainability in today's turbulent business climate. The path to your final destination has a logical sequence; a good road map will allow you to reach your goal with less hassle and frustration. This book explains essential rules and strategies that you will need in order to develop a simple, yet valuable "road map" to a successful business.

As an award-winning network marketer, internet marketing and social media expert, published author and accomplished platform speaker, I have met and coached many business owners over the years. When I first met Ed Klaameyer at one of my social media seminars, it was readily evident that he not only possessed a great business acumen, but he also revealed inspiring, real-life anecdotes.

I recall a conversation at a subsequent meeting when speaking about how families were struggling to make ends meet due to the economy. It was at this early stage of what grew into a solid friendship that I learned Ed "loves" to help others. He is especially supportive of sole-proprietor and small businesses since he started and developed several successful businesses during his professional career of over 40 years. There is nothing that gives him greater pleasure than helping someone transform a passion into a thriving business. Ed has been there and understands the struggles and the rewards of a successful business.

Every business will have differences, but when it comes to establishing a business strategy, certain rules and patterns must be followed. This book is a guideline for conducting research, compiling what you have learned and assembling a comprehensive and thorough plan. The situations that arise in business today vary greatly. However, this book explains the key elements that you should be aware of and will help unlock the door to a successful business.

The value of preparation cannot be overstated. The expert details and fundamentals found in "The Business Owner's Savings Bible" will help you bring out the best in yourself – in good and challenging times. There are two key components to achievement: extensive information and appropriate action. Not only does Ed provide the tools you will need to succeed in business, but he also provides business tips that are golden nuggets of knowledge to be used for your success.

Last but not least, Ed has provided 27 savings secrets your business can't survive without. This chapter is a MUST READ because it deals with "applied knowledge". While some of these secrets (27 small & home-based business tax deductions) are common knowledge, I have found that I am not taking advantage of #13, #18 & #25. This will help my bottom line at tax time!

I encourage any entrepreneur or executive to read this groundbreaking book and implement the principles that Ed Klaameyer has outlined and you will be empowered for success.

Larry C. Beacham Jr.

Founder of Larry Beacham, The Champion Builder

Author: Build a Team, Not a Downline

Message from the Author:

Thinking about starting a business? Every year, thousands of people catch the entrepreneurial spirit, so you are not alone. Entrepreneurialism has always been a guiding light for America; just look back at our history. Our country was founded and then settled by innovators willing to sacrifice old certainties for new opportunities. The people who came to America a few hundred years ago looking for a better life were risk takers in every sense.

Do not mistake being a risk taker with being reckless. Risk takers must also become risk analyzers – evaluating the pros and cons, then trusting their instincts and recognizing and seizing an opportunity to create their own businesses.

This book was written to aid risk takers in assessing if a hobby, a passion or an idea can be turned into a profitable business. As a business creator and entrepreneur for many years, I have recognized that smart and savvy business people have common traits that are keys to their success. I've highlighted comments, questions, ideas, thoughts and experiences in this book and hope you will apply these traits to your own strategy for success in making a truthful decision about starting, owning or managing a business.

Our lives are full of decisions. Even getting up in the morning is a decision! Every time a decision is made, there is a result – some good and some not-so-good. When forced to make a decision, you must have a choice.

I have over 40 years of professional experience in building several businesses into multi-million dollar companies. I even surrendered 15 of the best years of my life to an international corporation where I was provided sales quotas and it was my job to search out and cultivate target prospects and turn them into clients.

During this time, I was promoted and had to educate and teach others the very same system. Those 15 years were the best and worst of my life. I gained so much knowledge to make me a better professional, but I missed years of my kids growing up and being an integral part of their lives. The bottom line: all decisions will affect our lives, now and in the future.

What I tried to convey by writing this book is that one of the biggest and most important decisions you will ever make in your lifetime is the starting and running of a business. One of my startups took nearly two years to bring to an opening date. There were countless late evenings spent on the phone and on the computer. Having stated this and more to the positive side, there is great satisfaction in setting a launch date and then actually opening the doors.

In my travels, especially over the past 20 years, I have had conversations with many people around the country who had started or were running businesses that just did not develop as they had hoped or wished for. In my opinion, I perceive many of these folks had a great idea or a concept, but just did not prepare themselves, or their family, for what was required of time, money and expertise. In this book, I spend time diving into some of these key components that are necessary to gathering facts about a business and eventually formulate a sound business plan and build for the future.

Here are some guidelines to consider when you have to make important business decisions:

- Don't undersell yourself.

- Know that you are valuable and have abilities.

- Think about what you do well.

- Have goals for your life.

- Plan and take small action steps to reach your goal.

- Be the kind of person where nothing is lost. Some of the strongest and most intelligent business people often are the ones who have had tough breaks in their lives, but learned from them.

- Persevere.

- Be committed to what you know will help you in the future.

- Stay away from decisions that are made from your emotions.

- Look forward to tomorrow.

Further, decisions also have degrees of importance which affects everyone differently. What I deem as important may not affect you in the same way or with the same severity. Some decisions are made for us, or in other words, we can be a consequence of someone else's decision.

For example: Many years ago, I interviewed for a job along with 3 other job hunters. While waiting for my turn to be grilled by the interviewer, I had a conversation with one of the other applicants. He offered in our conversation that he had been out of work for 5 weeks and had yet to collect his first unemployment check.

By the tone of our conversation, I assumed that this fact had to be rough on him and the family because I later learned he also had two small children at home. My world would not come to an end if I was not offered that job, but certainly he had more to lose or gain. I did not get the job, so I prayed that he did. A decision was made to hire someone other than me and who knows, that may have turned out to be my "dream" job, but I will never know.

There are three levels of decisions –

Basic, Short-Term & Long-Term

LEVEL ONE: BASIC

Although some decisions can be extremely important, basic decisions generally do not have consequences that last for more than a few minutes up to a few days. Examples are: brushing hair, taking a shower or a bath, wear a green shirt or a blue one. For a student, it may be completing a homework assignment and so on. Personal hygiene or dining out are probably good examples of decisions we may make multiple times per day. The level of importance is considered – **LOW**.

LEVEL TWO: SHORT-TERM

Short-term decisions, when compared to a lifetime, can last a few days to a few weeks to a few years. These decisions can have far-reaching results, but in all cases, they come to an end at some future point in time.

The word "short" is a term that is relative to the decision being made. For a 50-year old, leasing a car for 30 months, is a short-term decision as compared to the number of years an adult will drive. For a 25-year old, this same lease term does not carry the same weight; due to a higher percentage of elapsed driving time compared to his age. For most adults, short-term decisions, whether the results are considered good or bad, may only last a few months to just a few years.

I made the conscious decision, at the age of 10, to lie about my age to obtain a paper route in my town. You see, you had to be 12 years of age and in the early 1960's, there were no background checks for paper boys. The vetting process consisted of a few questions from some guy in a paper delivery truck (he never asked my age, and I was only 11, not the required 12) and when I stated my birthday had just passed and I was ready to go to work --- I WAS IN! I sold myself so I could start earning money. I had this entrepreneurial spirit yearning in my soul and I never looked back. When compared to a lifetime, a short-term decision is time-definite.

The level of importance is considered – **LOW** to **MEDIUM**.

LEVEL THREE: LONG-TERM

Long-term decisions are of far greater importance and this is where vast amounts of procrastination can take place. Why? Due to several key factors, a long-term decision may affect every aspect of our life, and are not necessarily limited to the usual ones that come to mind like: an out-of-state move, a job, working for a certain employer, getting married, starting a family, buying a home, life insurance, a 401k or even the decision to start, own and build a business.

When considering turning a hobby into a business, or taking your years of experience in a certain discipline and starting a business, or just getting into a business because you just heard some smooth-talking presenter state he was making six-figures in 30 days, you have a BIG decision to make.

The level of importance is considered – **HIGH**.

We are all blessed with "free will" [free will \'frē- 'wil\ n : one's own choice or decision].

This book is divided into three sections:

Part I: Commitment, Passion, Desire & Motivation

I have always been in a business that catered to a customer or one somewhat related to the service industry. I started with a paper route, worked for an elderly woman in my town who needed help growing vegetables and weeding her garden (she made the best pies), to mowing lawns, baling hay & straw for a local farmer, pumping gas at a full-service gasoline station, repairing typewriters to drying off cars at a local car wash...all this before I turned 20 years old! I love helping other people and if this book can help just one person make a good decision, I am very happy.

This book will get into some of the most important aspects of starting or keeping a business going – keeping the doors open. Currently, I am involved with several business networking groups and I consistently see over 150 people each week, as an average. I can honestly say, some of these folks have told me they are not happy in their chosen profession. That is so sad because life is too short.

Part II: Definition, Customer Profile, Business Plan, S.W.O.T. & Roadblocks

To help with your decision-making process, this book will get into some deeper topics and in several of the chapters, you are provided with guidelines to follow that will help you make the best decision for you, your family and your future.

In my late 20's, after starting a family and a small business, I was turned down for a job teaching auto mechanics at a local high school. I really wanted this job but because I had no college experience, I was passed over. While at the time I felt my "real world" experience was enough to be handed the job at the highest pay grade, the reality was that I was not really prepared. So, in my late 20's, I set out to complete a college course of study – what a personal growth experience.

For readers who like numbers, a S.W.O.T. analysis is a key ingredient to finding out if a business has the "bones" to become a success or not. We will devote some pages to this topic. In college, I had taken a Business Strategies course and the S.W.O.T. analysis was one of the main concepts of study. In developing my businesses over the years, this type of analysis has been invaluable.

Part III: Savings Secrets, Tax Advantages, Business Tips

Your dream for true financial freedom can never be actualized if you still rely on your employer for a weekly paycheck. No one, but you can make your dream happen. No corporate organization provides real financial security, and the present situation of economies all over the world has made job security nothing but a mirage. Once you have read and absorbed Parts I & II of this book, you will be ready to put the "hammer down".

Now we get down to talking "business"! Let's put a strategy in place that will get you closer to your dream and include ways for your business to save money, provide for tax advantages and I will present business tips gained from years of experience. Remember that whatever your mind can conceive, you can always achieve it – your opportunities are limitless!

★ **Bonus Business Tip:**

Deductions create cash that you never have to pay back!

It is my sincere desire that you will find this book beneficial for your own entrepreneurial journey and adapt them to your own strategy for success. I hope you can apply them toward a new venture or use them in your existing business.

I've been discussing the different aspects of the decision-making process and by now you know that our daily lives are based on a series of basic, short-term & long-term decisions. Of course, as with any business endeavor, it does require your passion, commitment, support & determination. Business ownership can be very rewarding, but it will not necessarily be easy.

Once you learn and understand the information contained in this book, you will have the mindset to become successful. Once you have reached that level of achievement, you will then be able to pay it forward and educate others and help them make the best possible business decisions in their lives. I am confident that this book is your first step in helping you achieve your dream.

Make sure you look for the ★ throughout the book as this will identify a Bonus Business Tip that can save you thousands of dollars in business taxes.

Ed Klaameyer
Tampa, Florida

Table of Contents

CHAPTER ONE:

WHAT DOES IT TAKE TO SUCCEED?

Ask yourself this question: On a scale of 1 to 10 (10 as the highest), how high would I rate my desire to start or continue building a business?

CHAPTER ONE:

WHAT DOES IT TAKE TO SUCCEED?

I know that starting a business can be a little intimidating. Starting any business can be quite challenging and overwhelming, especially for those new to the business environment. This is due to the very fact that they are new to the terrain and are lacking in the knowledge of what it takes to become a successful business person. This problem is not only experienced by the new entrants into the business world, even the veterans do find the business environment overwhelming and challenging, too.

So the big question that new business people need to ask themselves is, "What does it really take to succeed in my chosen business?" Do I have the qualities to really succeed in this business? There are three basic entry options for getting into a business:

- Start a business from scratch

- Buy an existing business

- Purchase a franchise

Have you ever owned a business before? Well, this question has to be weighing on your mind, 24hrs a day & 7 days a week. The way to maximize your chances of success is to become familiar with the following key items identified for you.

Do I have what it takes to succeed in business?

To be a successful business person, generally speaking, you need to have a sound knowledge base of the business in question. There is no better recipe for failure than starting a business which you have little or no knowledge about.

Furthermore, you need to have the heart for the business, as well as possess the determination to ensure that you can take the business to a point of success. In addition, you need to exhibit many of the qualities discussed in this book if you ever hope to experience any form of success in your chosen business.

On the other hand, there are stories told of people who succeeded against all odds because they have an extremely strong desire to have their own business. This is not the norm. Founding your own business is unlike any other job you may take on. It's a pathway to a totally different lifestyle. You'll have to ask yourself whether you are ready for a complete commitment to the success of your business.

Burning desire for success

Success can only be achieved when you have a strong passion and drive to be successful. It is this desire that will propel you into making the desired efforts and sacrifices needed to ensure that success is achieved. Desire is the one element you must bring to the table. If you don't have it, no one can give it to you! Can you do it? Do you have the desire? It is pretty easy to want to own your own business, but "want" is only one criterion to consider before making the financial and emotional decision to move forward and start or continue running a business. There are five questions to ask yourself:

- Do I understand and accept the responsibilities of owning my own business?

- Will I enjoy my business?

- Do I have the personal attributes to be successful?

- Is there a financial commitment?

- Do I have family support?

Self-discipline

No business can be sustained in the long run if the business owner or the employees are lacking in discipline. You must be disciplined enough to know what to do with your time without necessarily being pushed or cajoled to spend it wisely. This also involves putting the required hours into your business, just as you would do if you were someone's employee. To be successful in your business, you must treat your business like a business and not like a hobby or part-time job.

Commitment

To be successful in your business, you need to be committed to achieving success with the business; this means going the extra mile to do all that is humanly possible. This may also mean committing some, or all of your financial resources into the business.

You must also be committed to your stated goals and objectives (we will get into this topic later). It involves staying true to those goals irrespective of the obstacles you might encounter along the way. Without commitment to your business, your dreams of achieving success or greatness with that business is just a fantasy.

> ## SAVINGS SECRET #1   HOME OFFICE DEDUCTION
>
> Measure your work area and divide by the square footage of your home. That percentage is the fraction of your home-related business expenses – rent, mortgage, insurance, electricity, etc. – you can claim.

Passion

A successful business cannot be built without having passion for the business. The passion you have for your business is what will keep you going on those days when nothing seems to be working appropriately and you might actually consider giving up on the business. When you are passionate about your business, achieving success becomes much easier because you will naturally channel your energy into the business to ensure its success.

Many entrepreneurs say the long hours they invest in growing their business do not feel like work because they're actually having fun in what they are doing. Passion is key for the success of your business. If you are not passionate or lack enthusiasm towards the business, you might as well call it quits and not go any further with the business idea or keeping the doors open. --- **STOP NOW!**

Self-belief & Pride

To achieve success in your business, you must have a strong belief in your ability, even when you experience temporary setbacks or failures. You need to believe that you have what it takes to succeed.

One of the biggest differences in owning your own company as opposed to working for someone else is the sense of pride you establish in building something of your own. Not only are there benefits from such self-actualization, but how about getting to brag about yourself once-in-a-while, too!

You can give back to your community

Many entrepreneurs love the idea when building their business, that they can give back to the communities where they live and work. This can be in the form of the products and services they offer, by donating to charities, and especially the ability to create jobs, which is particularly important these days.

Start-up Capital

Financing is important to the success of any business; therefore, it is best to have some funds available to kick start your business. I've attended presentations and heard people state they had started their business on a wing, a prayer and a Visa card. I hate to burst your bubble if you think this way, but those are the exceptions and not the rule.

Do I have the desire to own a business?

While it might sound obvious to say it, the desire to own a business is perhaps the most important element of owning a business. It is difficult to become a successful business entrepreneur if your only desire is to work for someone else and become a building block for their successful business. Anyone who is satisfied working for someone else will find the challenges of business ownership too great to even attempt.

While many people fantasize about being owners of a successful business, it is not everyone that has the potential to own one. Also, the few that do have potential, are those who are courageous enough to take that first step towards their financial independence.

Successful business owners are known to possess some distinct characteristics and these attributes are vital for their survival in the sometimes harsh and uncertain business environment. If you desire to own a business, you need to find out if it is the right occupation for you and if you have what it takes to make the business a success.

<u>SAVINGS SECRET #2</u>   ADVERTISING & MARKETING DEDUCTION

As long as they are directly related to your business, you can deduct the cost of ordinary advertising (business card purchases, yellow page ads, and so on), as well as promotion costs for good publicity (such as sponsoring a local sport team).

Provide your honest answers to these self-evaluation questions:

- **Positivity** - Are you passionate & motivated to become successful?
- **Proactive** - Are you the type of person who loves making things happen, or the laid back individual who likes to see others make things happen?
- **Determined** - Do you have well-defined and clearly-stated business and personal goals?
- **Hardworking** - Are you willing to put in all the necessary time the business requires?
- **Leader** - Do you have good leadership skills? Can you be a great example?   Can you get the best out of your subordinates?   Can you enforce discipline when necessary?
- **Opportunist** - Can you recognize opportunities and openings which may occur in your market every now and then?
- **Self-Critical** - Can you make an objective assessment of your performance?   How well do you take constructive criticism?
- **Flexible** - How flexible are you?   Can you change your methods quickly or easily if the market dictates a change?

While you don't necessarily have to satisfy all the requirements stated above, it is important that you satisfied most of them to be sure that you are adequately prepared for the challenge and hard work that starting and running your own business would demand.

If you are satisfied with your answers and you can accept the enormous responsibility to start and champion a business, you have to create your business plan, conduct some market research, get to know your type of customer and certainly have an idea of who your competitors are. This sort of information will help you make a well-guided decision on the chances of your business becoming successful. We dive into these topics later.

What is my primary motivation to own/run a business?

It is extremely important to know why you want to go into a business; this is because your motivation for owning or running a business will be your major reason for making the business a success.

It is essential that you have a reason for wanting to start or run a business. Your reason could be to create more time to spend with your kids, earn extra cash to pay down debt and create long-term wealth, or your motivation could be to take over your current employer's business and then turnaround and fire your boss.

Irrespective of your reason for wanting to own your own business, when you know and understand the purpose or motivation for starting that business, it gives you the driving force needed to make the business a success.

Other words that come to mind to describe the "why" or reason to own a business are drive, the desire for greater flexibility, control of one's future, financial success, independence, etc. In addition, it keeps you motivated and you will certainly gain a sense of purpose and direction.

There are many people who diligently built their business, became successful and still, they are unfulfilled and unsatisfied. Conversely, there are others who may not have attained or recorded any measurable success with their business, but they have a deep sense of fulfillment and satisfaction.

Your primary motivation for owning or running a business should go beyond just to make extra cash; **it should be centered on your beliefs, core values and desires**. You need to make an inward evaluation of your feelings and emotions to discover those key factors that are propelling you to start the business.

Your motivation is a strong driving force which can spur you to produce amazing results, help you make wise decisions or build a strong business relationship. This force, if well harnessed, will help you to become more efficient, skillful and could make your work as a business owner look more like playtime.

Furthermore, your primary motivation for owning a business will be the source of commitment, energy, vision and vitality needed to get the best you can out of life and build an incredible business for yourself. It will also propel you to take the necessary steps to attain a level of personal freedom.

Many people who try to build their business, home-based, network marketing or any kind of business without motivation, will usually quit long before they could achieve their set goals. Identification of your primary motivation for owning a business is a necessity if you are serious about deriving satisfaction and fulfillment from your business.

SAVINGS SECRET #3   **DEPRECIATION AS A TAX DEDUCTION**

If you buy property to use in your business, you generally can't deduct the entire cost in the year of purchase — but you can spread the cost over more than one tax year and deduct part of it each year.

What's in the next chapter?

Now that you have asked questions about desire, commitment, passion and motivation, in the next chapter we are going to look into your preferred business opportunity and clearly define what it is. Specifically, what sets your business apart from the competition, what your business does or will do better than the others. ▶

CHAPTER TWO:

IS THE BUSINESS A RIGHT FIT FOR ME?

If you don't follow your dreams, you will work for someone who did!

CHAPTER TWO:

IS THE BUSINESS A RIGHT FIT FOR ME?

Starting a business can be a daunting task, though it can be very rewarding. Suffice it to say, the initial stage is usually filled with difficulties, BUT not insurmountable. Though some people already know the right business venture they would like to start or leap into, but for most people, it is not so easy. The BIG question to be answered is, which is the right one?

If considering a business venture, it is likely that you have struggled or are struggling within yourself about making the right decision.

If you are considering a franchise, home-based or online business, there are thousands of choices and you could end up getting confused. What is the right choice?

To be successful in any business you need to be sure it is something you really have passion for. It is the passion that will help you push the business through the long hours and the difficult responsibilities. Therefore, in deciding if a business is the right fit, you need to consider what you are passionate about and what is your knowledge base.

You have to know your business

I am sure you have heard some say, "I wish I owned that business. It is a sure thing." Well, my advice to you is that you don't take that comment to heart. Nothing in business is a sure thing. Nearly every day when you open your mailbox, there is always one piece or more of "junk mail" that you throw away or recycle if you are an eco-conscience person.

Many years ago, I started a postal processing business where I would mail "tons" of non-time sensitive mail all over the world for my clients. It was a "sure thing" that the United States Postal Service would never fall into economic hard times. Who would have dreamed that the US Postal Service would run into serious money problems during the '80's and '90's and lose thousands upon thousands of customers? There is never a "sure thing". Every business is filled with risks; some more than others. You are better off starting a business which closely matches your personality, a business based on your knowledge, skills and interests.

If you already have work experience in your field and have first-hand knowledge about a business, you might consider starting out in that industry because of the advantages you will enjoy. If you happen to possess many interests and you are not sure of the one that would be your best choice, then you must consider which skill sets are your strongest.

Also, your educational background, training and other industry-specific qualifications will help you decide the business best suited for you or visa-versa. More on this later.

Keep reading, because this book will provide plenty of good information so you make the best decision possible – which may well be: "Do I really want to start a business?"

Think About It

On the average, you spend 40 hours per week at your working place. Assuming you start working at the age of 20 and you retire at 64, you would have spent about 90,000 hours working. That's a considerable amount of hours, but it is actually nothing when compared to the hours you will need to work when running your own business.

Running a successful business is a huge demand on your time. That is all the more reason why you need to start a business you truly have a passion for. Your business has a higher chance of success if it is something you naturally love and the long hours you will need to put in will be inconsequential. Work becomes play when you love your vocation and are building for the future.

Is your business compatible with you?

You need to know if a business is compatible with you. In other words, make sure the business is a good fit for you prior to committing your energy, your time and your money (probably loans, too).

SAVINGS SECRET #4   AUTO MAINTENANCE
TAX DEDUCTION

If you own the vehicle, the most common method is known to the IRS as an accountable plan, which is akin to an expense account. You drive your vehicle for work purposes, keep track of the costs incurred while doing so and seek reimbursement. We're talking about tolls, parking, gas, car washes, mileage, maintenance and repairs. Sorry, but the tax code does not permit deductions for commuting to work, which is considered a personal use.

The following steps will help you assess if your proposed business is the right one for you. There are many more factors you can consider, but this is a great beginning:

1. Try out the business

It is always a good idea that you try getting some experience or training in your industry or business of interest. If you can manage economically, taking an entry level position is always an option. Does your industry have any non-profit organizations where you can volunteer for the short-term? Learn all you can about all the aspects of your business.

2. Talk to entrepreneurs in the same field

If it is a business you are not very familiar with, you will want to talk to others who are in the industry. You may even need to travel to a different geographic area or location to speak with people in the trade. Many entrepreneurial business owners will share their knowledge freely with you once they are assured that you are not competing with them, so you will want to assure them that you are not "poaching" their customers.

3. Evaluate whether you enjoy the work and excel at it.

Do you enjoy the work? Do you derive satisfaction and sense of fulfillment from the business? If the business is something you enjoy and you have the skill set to excel at it, then it could be a correct business for you.

4. Judge your ability and desire to handle every aspect of the business.

You need to be able to judge if you can effectively manage every angle of the business. Can you manage the challenges and the frustration that might come your way? Do you have what it takes to be an entrepreneur? Do you have the risk-taking spirit?

5. Determine whether the business has a chance of turning a profit.

Though money is not the sole reason why you enter into business or continue to run or manage a business, you probably do not have a desire to run a charity organization either. The business should be a potential money maker.

Here are two key items for you to think about: will your business or does your current business meet both your personal and business obligations? You need to know the profit potential of the business or at least get as close to profit numbers as you can.

If you are going to be running at a loss or break even, there is no sense in starting a business with little or no profit potential. Makes sense to me! If you cannot derive the money to compensate yourself for the time and effort you are putting into the business, then you need to reevaluate your objectives. The business must be in alignment with both your personal and professional financial goals.

Summary

The process of starting a business can be frightening and exciting at the same time. Starting or managing a business can be challenging, but can also be filled with many good moments. No one makes a serious decision without getting a little nervous or at least have some sleepless nights. If you don't get nervous, you may not know enough!

In the end, the decision to continue or to start a business is entirely up to you. The more time you put into planning and preparation, the better your chances of attaining success are. Good, solid, serious research and good advisers will lead you to a good decision.

Talk to the successful business owners -- they're the ones who can give you the most information on how to succeed in business. Also if you can, be sure to talk to the unsuccessful owners and learn from them. Find out what they would have done differently to avoid making a bad decision.

When you have gathered the information and are honest about your own abilities, you will make a smart, educated decision for yourself…despite the butterflies!

EXPECT TO GET NERVOUS,
BUT DON'T LET NERVES STEAL YOUR DREAM

In the final analysis, the businesses that succeed are almost always the ones run by people who love and are passionate about what they do. Find something you are passionate about and find a smart way to implement it.

What's in the next chapter?

Now that you have matched your business opportunity with your personality, skills, interests and qualifications, let's clearly define your business in the next chapter. ▶

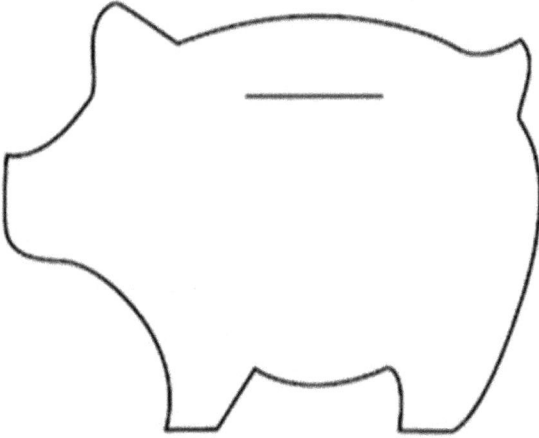

CHAPTER THREE:

DEFINING THE BUSINESS

Learn everything you can about the business you want to start and the marketplace you'll be operating in. This means getting work experience and collecting information so you'll know the industry inside and out.

CHAPTER THREE:

DEFINING THE BUSINESS

A business definition is one of the most important factors that will make for a successful enterprise. It is a necessity and vital for the growth of your business which must not be overlooked. When the business is properly defined, it will provide answers to some of the most significant issues that need to be addressed if your business is to become successful.

You need to offer satisfactory answers to pertinent questions such as who are you? What is the objective or the primary focus of your business? Why is your business unique? Why should people patronize you? All these questions need to be properly addressed if you are to become successful in your business. Defining your business also helps you to remain focused and make judicious use of your resources.

What Do You Do?

It is important that you clearly define the primary function or the core area of your business so that you do not find yourself veering off of the pathway to your primary goal. Your main focus should be on the primary goal(s); while it is true that you can diversify your business, it is much more important to concentrate on your main or primary goal, especially if you are just starting out. Identity development is crucial to a business, especially for a new entity.

Your business should have a main focus and if there is anything else you uncover along the way; you can always develop those ideas later on down the road. Consider it to be just a subheading or subsidiary of the main area of focus. Have a clearly defined business definition and pursue it vigorously.

★ **Bonus Business Tip:**

For every 100 business miles driven at $0.54 per mile = $54.00 for an auto mileage tax deduction. At a 33% tax bracket = $17.82 cash savings. (using the IRS Mileage Rate Method)

SAVINGS SECRET #5   AUTO MILEAGE
TAX DEDUCTION

If you drive for business, the IRS wants to give you some money back. The IRS loves documentation, so keep a notebook in your vehicle to record the date, mileage, tolls, parking costs and the purpose of your trip. At the end of the year, you have two choices. You can total the mileage and add in the tolls and parking to calculate your deduction. Or you can measure your business usage against your personal driving and deduct that portion of your auto-related expenses. (include gas, repairs and insurance)

What Sets You Apart?

You need to openly define what sets your business apart from others in your field -- what makes you different or unique? If you can provide a satisfactory answer to this, it should be a stronghold for your marketing campaigns to blow competing businesses away. You should let the public know why you are unique; let them know why you are the best. Give them a good reason why they need to do business with you and not your competition.

Why We Should Buy from You?

You need to let people know what they stand to gain by patronizing you. In this case, you need to think more like a customer. When you are marketing, advertising or promoting the business, put yourself in the shoes of the customer. It is only when you can convince buyers that you know more than they do about your service or product, or you offer enough value to meet their need, that they will be willing to part with their money. In other words, they want to buy what you are selling.

This will go a long way to helping established your business identity. Since all we want is to be attractive to the customers, play with different ideas and try out new things on Facebook® or some other social media site, until you get it right. Have you heard the expression, "I feel your pain"? Does your product or service relieve a prospect's pain? If you can find that "pain point", use this as a marketing strategy to convert your prospects into customers or buyers. Think about this very simple concept: once you can market your product or service as a way to relieve someone's "pain", your business will take off like a rocket!

What Is Your 30-second Infomercial?

As I mentioned at the beginning of this book, I am a member of several networking groups and I see, on average, about 150 people on a regular basis each and every week. If you know anything about networking, you must have a 30-second infomercial that will describe your business AND pique someone's interest in either becoming a customer of yours or referring your business to their customers or business contacts.

In other words, an infomercial screams, "DON'T WASTE MY TIME – JUST GIVE ME THE FACTS ABOUT YOUR BUSINESS AND GET TO THE POINT!"

Many folks really miss the mark on this subject. I've been to numerous sales training workshops over my 40-year professional career, and in almost every session, the key must-have items drilled into us for the creation of an "awesome introduction" or 30-second infomercial are:

- Who am I?

- What is my target audience?

- What is their "pain"?

- How can I help relieve their "pain"?

- What is the expected outcome my product or service will deliver?

Here is a real-life example of a 30-second infomercial:

Hi, my name is William Smith, but call me Bill.

I represent "Smith Business Coaching".

I educate and train small business owners to attract new clients through social media and traditional media outlets.

I am an author and business coach with a proven prospect-to-customer conversion model.

Build your business through my customer-attraction techniques the same way thousands of my readers have.

Bill Smith of Smith Business Coaching.

◆————————————————————————◆

Now, if I was in the market for a business coach, Bill has provided all the necessary information for me to make an informed decision about his skill set. Even if I was not in need of his services at this time, I know enough about him that I would feel comfortable enough to refer him to any one of my clients.

SAVINGS SECRET #6   UTILITIES DEDUCTION

The water, power, trash, and telephone bills at your office are all 100 percent deductible as regular business expenses. If you have a phone line that has a mix of business and personal calls, highlight the business calls and deduct only the business related portion of the bill.

Your 30-second infomercial template

Hi, my name is _____

I represent _____

(I or my company) help _____

to _____

_____

(I or my company)

_____

With (me or my company) you get the expected results

_____

Name & company name

_____

What Do You Do Best?

Everybody has their area of core competency, strong points or skill set. You need to know what your strengths are, focus on them and promote them. Your customers will then be able to associate their need with your strong suit. Your strengths will benefit your business by creating brand recognition and this is a key factor in creating your business definition. There is more about strengths and weaknesses (**SWOT**) later in this book.

Others Perceptions

Through a business definition, your customers should see you as a credible person, trustworthy, responsible, accountable, dependable, reliable and that you possess many more attributes. As your customers or prospects become more at ease with you, they will begin to see that you are an expert in your field and this will help in strengthening your business brand.

Finally, there are three elements that should be contained in a business definition: a definition addresses your proposed market (i.e. who it is serving), the products or the service being rendered and the problem it will solve (i.e. what is the pain point). While defining your business may not be easy, it will certainly help your enterprise become more successful.

So, spend as much time as necessary to come up with the best definition of your business.

Is there a proven business system to follow?

For those people who may be thinking about a franchise, this needs to be an essential principle for you to think about. There are many dynamics at work when it comes to running a successful franchise. Obviously, all franchise systems are not the same, and every business has distinguishing features which sets it apart from the others. Please be sensitive to the fact that there are certain fundamental principles which can be applied to any franchise business or if you are considering buying an established business. The goal must be to obtain a successful return on any type of business.

A business system generally consists of a total package for running the business: location, marketing products, sales process, management and training.

Some say it is even more important than having a great product! In addition to a franchise business, a system can be applied to home-based or network marketing businesses (more about home-based & network marketing businesses in another book). Any reputable and successful franchise is all about a business system. If you really desire to run a successful franchise, then you need to follow a tested and proven system. Don't try re-inventing the franchise system because you will surely become frustrated and quite often will end up at odds with your franchisor.

PUT AS MUCH EMPHASIS AS YOU CAN in determining the system that is "appropriate" for you. That's right; this is where **you** become the most important part of seeking out a franchise! No matter how good the business system is, the business must be one that suits you.

Many years ago, I owned a service station with full-service gasoline pumps, auto and truck mechanics and believe it or not, in those days we repaired cars and trucks! I'm giving away my age, but some of us remember our local service station as a place to buy tires, have your oil changed and even have someone pump your gas!

The point here is, I was building a business around my passion at the time – cars. As a retail business, I represented a national gasoline company that had a proven system. This brand had been in business for many years and it had name recognition (they did all the advertising and marketing). The brand had a proven marketing program that sponsored and advertised their products to all the big name auto racing drivers of the time. Well guess what, my service station was only a few miles from a sports car racing track that drew in people from all over the country. For the big races, we took advantage of the name recognition during our promotions and our sales went through the roof!

As cars became more sophisticated and complex, we kept up with the necessary training offered by the company. Certifications for mechanics was just coming into vogue, so if I was going to continue to grow the mechanical part of the business, I had to make sure my mechanics were put through the certification process.

Thankfully, a large component of the proven system dealt with and offered education and training. At the time, auto emissions testing and regulations were mandated by the federal government, so training was a huge part of our continued existence in the auto repair business.

We've all heard the expression, "Location, Location, Location" and this was so true for my service station. Good franchisors know the demographics required to support their business. If it is a business where location is important, you should expect the franchisor to provide assistance in finding the best location. It was no accident that the location for my service station was at the intersection of two major highways. You can't have cars without a highway and since my target market were car owners, it does not take a rocket scientist to figure out the importance of my location.

The next segment for your consideration is the accounting or the paperwork portion of a business. Yes, there is the dreaded documentation. Any business system worth researching is going to have an accounting or bookkeeping component. This system should have all the forms, software programs and all the requirements to carry forward the business model. Even back in the late 70's and early 80's there were federal and state regulations as applied to the tax laws of the time for my industry. Accounting was extremely important.

So, an important decision for me was to make sure I had both a bookkeeper and a certified public accountant (CPA) to ensure that my business followed the letter of the law. My love and passion was helping customers and I was smart enough to realize that paperwork was better handled by others.

I have provided you with some of my personal experiences, but there are franchise regulations in place for the benefit of a person considering buying a franchise. As of December, 2015, federal law and state laws in 14 states, require that a franchise prospect receive a current copy of a document known as the Franchise Disclosure Document (FDD).

A proven business system to emulate should:

- have a record of people who have used the system to obtain the results you desire.

- have been operational for a minimum of 2-5 years. The first few years can be shaky and quite frequently are unstable, but during the second year you should start to see growth in most areas of the business. Once through the second year and into the third, a system that survived those years is a proven system.

- be predictable to a certain extent. Trends will develop over a period of time and the developments will make the system predictable. This is a good thing.

- be innovative in terms of operations and service development or products. The business should display signs of growth and become more dynamic.

- have a system which helps protect you and your business from becoming overrun by competition in the marketplace. A franchisor will want to protect the investment.

- allow for your individual creativity.

No matter how good the business system is, the business must be one that "matches" you. It must be a business system that builds on your strengths and talents. A system does not run by itself. Another important consideration for a business is personal preferences. Thinking about your personal business preferences will help you to identify how various businesses will fit your type of management style. While business goals tend to be universal, business preferences tend to be very personal.

After you read through this book, you will have the ability to identify a business that fits your profile. It is very difficult to be successful in a home-based, franchise, and to a lesser extent an online business, if there is no proven plan. In other words, you have a very low chance of achieving success.

Success often leaves clues behind and when you find someone who has travelled the road leading to success and is willing to share their experiences with you, then you will become better equipped for success. In all likelihood, a person who is looking to bring you into a business, should be willing to share, not only their own success stories, but refer others to you as a part of your research; and if not, then run as far away as you can!

SAVINGS SECRET #8   TAX DEDUCTION
EQUIPMENT REPAIRS

The cost of repairs to keep your business equipment in operating condition can be taken as a deduction.

What's in the next chapter?

Moving your business into a new market - where to begin. ▶

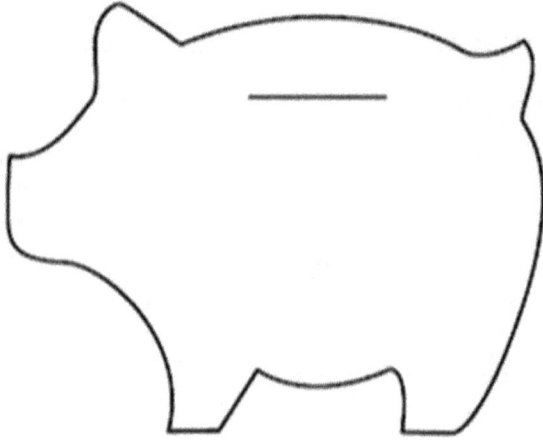

CHAPTER FOUR:

PROVEN BUSINESS IN A NEW MARKET

Ask yourself this question: Will my product(s) or service(s) relieve my customers' pain?

CHAPTER FOUR:

PROVEN BUSINESS IN A NEW MARKET

The entrepreneur or business owner has to establish the position of the business in the market place. Taking an established product or business to a new market may sound wonderful, but there are risks attached to it. It is far easier to be successful in your current market because the product is already established and you are very familiar with the needs of the customer base. Your enterprise has been promoted tirelessly, marketed extensively and has now developed into a mature business.

But moving to a new market is an entirely different experience. You are just a new face in the market and you need to prove yourself. You now have new customers to provide a service or a product to, and yes, new competitors to be aware of, as well.

Therefore, you must be ever mindful that while expanding your proven business into a new market, you have to understand the importance of proceeding into the new market with caution, even though you should be enthusiastic to some degree.

Since the business has been proven and succeeded in one market, it should give you a good idea of what is required to make the business a success in the new marketplace. In addition, you already have a product or service to render and you have probably put a distribution channel in place, so you are not really starting everything from scratch. You only need to replicate what led to your success in the original market.

However, you need to consider both the benefits and problems that the new market may present to you. Taking a proven business into a new market may be advantageous to you, since you already have a good understanding of the customer in the old market. Essentially, you only need to leverage on those lessons that were learned and grow your customer base.

When taking a proven business into a new market, you may need to change the way you do some things in order to meet the specific needs of a portion of your new customers. You must be prepared to change if you really want to succeed. This is where your customer service skills come into play.

SAVINGS SECRET #9   TAX DEDUCTION - LICENSES

License fees, as well as regulatory fees, are deductible.

Moving into a new market, customer service has to be a top priority. Listen to what the new customers are saying, because If you are not prepared to introduce any necessary changes to your method of operation, then you might need to target a different set of customers.

There is an essential need for you to carefully examine your product or service to find out if there are certain categories of customers that you did not promote to previously. Spend time asking questions or performing surveys to try and find out what are the best ways to attract these new customers.

It is easier for you to make an inroad into a new market when you are able to identify new groups of possible customers. In order to identify your potential markets, you need to identify those who are currently buying your service or product or maybe, what are they actually buying? What particular customer needs are you meeting? What is the "pain point" of your new prospective customer base?

Then you do some thinking; ask yourself if there are other groups that can benefit from your service or product. Ask yourself, are there changes to introduce into packaging your service or product that will attract new groups of customers?

Moving into a new market is almost like starting a business all over again. Launching a proven business into a new market can be quite challenging; nevertheless, success can be attained in the new market if you approach it with due diligence and you are sure that there is demand for the product. Have you completed your market research? Demand is the key.

Acknowledge the competition & describe how your company differs from the others.

When your business differentiation is thoroughly and thoughtfully defined, it will go a long way to help you identify who you are, what service you render and why you are different. While many business owners do not care to provide answers to these questions, you need to answer them because they are important for creating a strong identity.

Also, this will help your business make a stronger impression on your targeted customers. When your business is properly differentiated from the crowd, your customers are in a better position to remember you when they have a demand for your product or service. The importance of name recognition depends on the industry, but in consumer-oriented businesses, it is often what separates the successful ones from all of the others.

SAVINGS SECRET #10   TAX DEDUCTION FOR OFFICE SUPPLIES

Pens, paper, staples, thumb tacks... keep those receipts!

To properly outline the difference in your business, there is need for you to determine the characteristics of your business.

- Who are you?

- What is the nature of your business?

- What is your mission?

- Do your products or services offer value?

- What are the unique services or products you offer?

Study and compare your business to the competition

Identify your competition

- Who provides the same service or products?
- Who are you directly competing against?
- In other words, who are your closest rival or rivals?
- Are there any secondary market competitor(s) you could be facing in the future?

When formulating your business definition, your competitors (closest rivals) are ones you should target in your definition.

This bears repeating: it is suggested that you conduct research about similar businesses that are successful and note what they are doing and apply the same principles to your business.

What Makes You Different

Establish how and why your business is different from your competitors. Do you have a particular area of specialization either in your chosen market or the product or service you provide? Do you serve a particular geographic area that is ignored by others? If possible, identify a niche. Usually the niche or opportunity will be an innovation or proven idea in a new market or a unique idea in an existing market.

When differentiating your business, always avoid using expressions that include: faster, better, or cheaper. Why? Over time your business will grow and then these terms will become too subjective for your brand. The differentiators of your business should stick with the business throughout the lifetime of the business.

★Bonus Business Tip:

Meals & Entertainment deductions are possible if:

#1. You are running your business like a business.
   (you may need to offer proof, if called in for an audit)

#2. The reason for claiming this deduction is the promotion of business in pursuit of a profit. (you do not have to close a sale, just the pursuit of the sale)

What's in the next chapter?

What are the strengths and weaknesses of your business? ▶

CHAPTER FIVE:

LIST THE STRENGTHS & WEAKNESSES

After you read through this book, you will have the ability to
identify a business that fits your profile.

CHAPTER FIVE:

STRENGTHS AND WEAKNESSES OF THE BUSINESS

As an entrepreneur, you will encounter different challenges which you must be ready to battle head–on. The business environment is endlessly dynamic, and your competitors are constantly planning and implementing a strategy about how to acquire a greater share of the market. You need to have a well-planned strategy that will catapult your business to success ahead of your competition.

You need to understand your business and identify those things which can enhance or hinder your success. A **SWOT** analysis of your business is the right tool you can use to achieve a greater chance for success and increase the marketability of your products or services.

A **SWOT** analysis will help you identify what strengths you can build upon. It will also identify what needs to change, the opportunities available to you and the factors that can hinder you from achieving success in your business.

I have personally used this business tool multiple times and it never ceases to amaze me how something this simple can provide so much information about a business.

The information obtained from a **SWOT** analysis can be used to fine-tune sales presentations, advertising and marketing strategies, customer service, employee training programs and so much more.

The acronym **SWOT** means: **S**trengths, **W**eaknesses, **O**pportunities and **T**hreats

S.W.O.T. ANALYSIS

To know the strengths, weaknesses, opportunities and threats of your business, you need to identify the following aspects of your business:

Strengths

- What is it that you do well?
- What can you do better than others?
- What resources do you have?
- What advantages do you have over your competition?
- What are the major factors responsible for your past success?

Weaknesses

- What needs to be improved in your business?
- Where do you have lesser resources compared to your competition?
- What might others perceive as your weaknesses?
- What are the major factors responsible for your past success failures?

Opportunities

- What are the opportunities available to you?
- What are the trends/changes in the business environment?
- What opportunities do those trends or changes present?
- How can your strengths be changed into opportunities?

Threats

- Who is your real competition?
- What is your competition doing that you should be concerned about?
- What are the challenges you are facing?

SWOT analysis is a powerful model for many different situations. The **SWOT** tool is not just for business and marketing.

Here are some examples of what a **SWOT** analysis can be used to assess:

- a company (its position in the market, commercial viability, etc.)

- a method of sales distribution

- a product or brand

- a business idea

- a strategic option, such as entering a new market or launching a new product

- changing a supplier

- outsourcing a service, activity or resource

- project planning and project management

- an investment opportunity

- personal financial planning

- personal career development - direction, choice, change, etc.

- education and qualifications planning and decision-making

- life-change - downshifting, relocation,

- relationships, perhaps even family planning?

Whatever the application, be sure to clearly describe the subject (or purpose or question) for the **SWOT** analysis so you remain focused on the central issue. This is especially crucial when others are involved in the process. People contributing to the analysis and seeing the finished **SWOT** analysis must be able to properly understand the purpose of the **SWOT** assessment and the internal / external implications resulting from the exercise.

See S.W.O.T. worksheet on next page...

SWOT ANALYSIS WORKSHEET

	Positive	Negative
	STRENGTHS	**WEAKNESSES**
I N T E R N A L	Advantages Capabilities Resources Assets People	Lack of cometitive strength Financials Our vulnerabilities Timestables Deadlines Pressures Continuity Processes Systems
	OPPORTUNITIES	**THREATS**
E X T E R N A L	Market developments Business development Product development Service development	Environmental effects Market demand(s) Obstacles

The Business Owner's Savings Bible_SWOT

What's in the next chapter?

It's all about the customers. Who is a customer, what do they want, how often will they make a purchase and where are the customers located? ▶

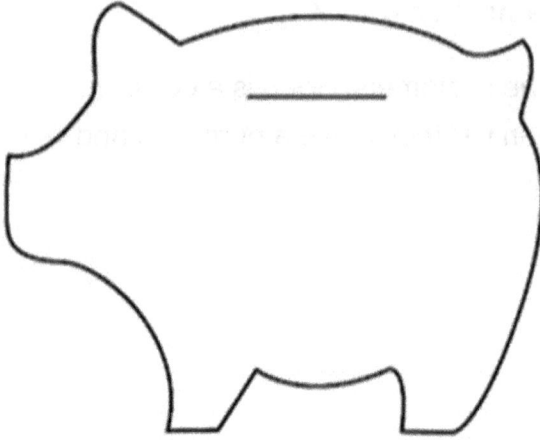

CHAPTER SIX:

IDENTIFY THE IMPORTANT GROUPS OF CUSTOMERS

With the segmentation of your customers, you will be able to separate your marketing messages and create effective messages that will address the needs of a particular group and push them to take action?

CHAPTER SIX:

IDENTIFY THE IMPORTANT GROUPS OF CUSTOMERS

Having a good understanding of those who constitute your customer base is essential for the success of any business whether you are a startup or a mature business. Suffice it to say, a new or startup business has to put more emphasis on the customer.

The understanding of your customer base is not just important for you to be able to make sound decisions on the type of product or service to render; you also need to have a good understanding of your customer base as it affects the packaging, pricing, and the promotion of your products or services.

The demographics of your customer is one tool you can use as leverage to identify the potential market for your business. With the demographic information, you will be able to identify both your present and future customers, where they reside, and the probability of them buying your product or services.

You can also easily identify the changing needs of the market and adjusting accordingly through studying the demographics of the customers. As a business owner, your ability to identify the demographic group that will have the most interest in your service or product might be the difference between you becoming successful or failing, especially since you cannot afford to make errors like the big companies. See more about demographics in the Target Marketing section.

The demographic information is desirable for two basic reasons; it is needed to analyze the characteristics of the population so that you are able to really know who your potential customer is. Also, demographic information is used to identify the geographical locations where your potential customers are predominantly concentrated.

For instance, if your business interest is in marketing a denture cream, you would most likely be interested in knowing the cities which have the highest percentage of elderly users.

After you have identified the states, counties or cities, next you will want to obtain additional information about those elderly people. Information such as, how many of them wear dentures, their purchasing habits, their income and many more statistics that will be important for you to know.

**SAVINGS SECRET #12   TRAVEL EXPENSE
                         TAX DEDUCTION**

Nearly all business travel expenses are 100 percent deductible. These include airfare, hotels, and other on-the-road expenses (like dry cleaning, Wi-Fi or cab fares). Eating out on the road is also deductible, but only up to 50 percent.

In years past, mass marketing was the major method utilized in the selling of goods and services. Mass marketing simply involved the use of radio, television and newspapers to reach to the potential customer. The focus of mass marketing systems was not prone to locating a targeted market or customers, it was more of getting your product or service to as many people as possible.

Of course, the result of this method was quite glaring; companies and business owners were spending huge sums of money to reach potential customers without any guarantee that any of the audience reached really needed the services or products being pushed at them. While mass marketing still remains an important medium of reaching a potential market, most businesses have now come to the realization that it is not necessarily a cost-effective medium for selling one's service or product.

Bonus Business Tip:

Deduct 50% of entertainment expense if you talk business in the same 24-hour day… (i.e. lunch and then a baseball game)

TARGET MARKETING

With the decline of using mass marketing as a tool for reaching the customer, targeted marketing has become the order of the day. Targeted marketing involves obtaining all the possible information you can about both your present and possible future customers; then devising special marketing or advertising campaigns to reach them.

When you know your customer better, you will begin to discover that they have certain traits and characteristics which may be common to some of them, thereby helping to easily separate or classify them into various segments. Over time and with some analysis, the difference between the different segments of your customers will begin to emerge.

A segment of your important customers may be women; one of your products might be popular among married adult men, while career women might form the nucleus of the buyers of another product. The segmentation of the different profiles is endless.

Though the segmentation of customers is different from one business to another, in most cases, there are four main segments that you need to consider: demographic, geography, behavior and lifestyles. The proper categorization of your customers will ensure that your marketing efforts become effective since your message will be based on what a particular segment needs or wants.

Demographic

Demographic segmentation involves separating your customers into different groups based on their age, gender, income, ethnicity, race, education level, family size, ages of children, location, occupation etc.

The analysis of the demographic data is exceptionally vital to the success of your business. For instance, a concept that is widely accepted is that a person's income will generally increase with age.

Over time, people will get a better paying job which will positively influence the patronage of your product or services. Also, younger people have lesser purchasing powers than their older counterparts. Lastly, a person that is well educated will most likely earn a greater income and definitely possess more disposable income to buy your products or services.

SAVINGS SECRET #13   **INTEREST EXPENSE TAX DEDUCTION**

Mortgage interest and finance charges or fees. Interest on payment plans, and interest paid on other loans are all 100 percent tax deductible.

Behavior

You can also segment your customers according to their buying behavior. This involves separating them into **frequency**, or how often they may buy from you. For example, weekly, monthly, and maybe only on a yearly basis.

For your information, loyalty programs are one of the best ways to reward customers for their patronage and acknowledge frequency. For example, there are programs based on smart cards that will enable small and mid-sized businesses to issue and redeem electronic gift and loyalty cards, with programs tailored to an individual merchant's needs. Merchants can increase customer loyalty and build store traffic by offering frequency points, points for purchases and rebates on purchases, all of which can be implemented and tracked through the program.

When you are able to divide your customers based on their buying behavior, it will help you to create and send the relevant marketing messages to them. You may want to get closer to the ones buying less frequently from you while at the same time maintaining a solid relationship with your regular customers.

Segmenting your customers according to their behavior is important; it enables you to approach every customer in the most suitable way. Don't forget to identify the "pain points" of each sector or division of buyers.

Geography

Geographical separation of your customers simply involves segmenting your customers by location or **geography**. Depending on your resources and where you have determined your target customers are located, the data used is generally based on their state, county, city or local area.

The geographical location of your customers can be an important factor in determining the type of products or service they will buy from you. When you are trying to determine who your potential customer is, look at your existing customer base in your current geographic location.

★**Bonus Business Tip:**

With a home office deduction, you may claim portions of: utilities, home interest, taxes, depreciation, security service, cleaning service, rent plus much more.

SAVINGS SECRET #14   TAX DEDUCTION FOR SOFTWARE

Boxed or downloaded software are included. With more software being made available as a service, software subscriptions are also tax deductible.

The following challenge questions will help you determine the best geographic area to promote and market your business:

- **Where do your inquiries come from?** Inquiries are people that are ready to become customers if you have what they want. Following up on inquiries can give you a targeted geographic area. This information is correlated to let the store know where customers are coming from and it quickly provides you with a targeted geographic market to expand into.

- **Where do non-customers live?** Determine the geographic area where people who fit your customer profile live, but who have not purchased from you. These are potential customers.

- **Do publications have the demographic information you need?** Publications that serve your market both conduct research and purchase research. Many times they share this information in an effort to get you to buy their services. Of course, you can also purchase this information from market research companies as well.

- **Can your industry association help?** If you are a member of any industry-related associations or organizations, they will likely have a great deal of market analysis that can help you determine the best geographical area suited to expansion.

- **Have you used the Internet to analyze your best geographic expansion?** This is one of the best sources for information available at little to no cost.

Lifestyles

The division of your customers according to **lifestyles** allows you to group them by their values, religion, attitudes, hobbies, religious backgrounds and beliefs, cultural backgrounds, political convictions, eating habits, recreational activities/ hobbies etc. The list is almost endless when segmenting prospective customers by lifestyles.

SAVINGS SECRET #15   CHARITABLE CONTRIBUTIONS DEDUCTION

If you contribute $250 or more, and claim the deduction, you need to have a letter from the organization which verifies your donation. To figure out how much you can deduct with non-monetary donations, see IRS Publication 561, Determining the Value of Donated Property.

Summary

Take time to diligently analyze the specifics common to your customers, irrespective of their groups or section you divided them into. With the splitting up of your customers, you will be able to separate your marketing messages and create effective postings, promotions and messages that will address the needs of a particular group and push them to take action.

Being able to separate your prospects and customers affects almost every aspect of a business from sales, marketing, advertising, product development and so much more. You may want to promote your business through several efficient and cost-effective methods. Have I mentioned that you must identify a prospects "pain point?" Here are some other ideas:

- Coupons generate traffic and reward a customer visit.

- On-hold phone messages educate and inform prospects and customers about your products and services while they wait to speak to a representative.

- Articles and press releases about your business submitted to magazines, newspapers, business journals, chambers of commerce can be great ways to broaden your exposure.

- Networking through leads groups, local chambers of commerce, rotary clubs and so on help promote your business in your local community.

- Event sponsorship can get your business's name in front of your local community and enhance your reputation as a concerned and caring neighbor.

- Promotional items (such as pens, pencils and coffee cups) printed with your company logo can help customers and prospects remember who you are and what you offer.

- Free link exchanges with other websites bring visitors from other sites to yours.

- Search engine optimization can help increase your website ranking.

SOCIAL MEDIA

Social media is the term commonly given to Internet and mobile-based channels and tools that allow users to interact with each other and share opinions and content. As the name implies, social media involves the building of communities or networks and encouraging participation and engagement.

Success in social media is not so much about the different social networks, but your strategy for how to use them. To apply them effectively for communications, we have to recognize that socializing online is all about participation in discussions and sharing of ideas and content. You've heard it soundly stated many times before: social media is where it's at when it comes to promoting your business. It can increase public awareness of your brand, foster a connection with your customers and improve your search engine ranking.

But how exactly can you achieve these results when you're just starting out? After all, it certainly feels like an uphill battle when you're struggling to gain interest in your business. There are hordes of books that have been written on this subject for small businesses. In fact, just browse through your local bookstore and you will see stacks of books dealing with this very important subject.

While I am not going to expand too much on this subject, I would be remiss if I did not mention some <u>social media key points</u> to be aware of:

- There is a <u>proven value</u> by using social media for businesses

- Only focus on <u>one or two social networks</u> that best suit your needs

- <u>Content is key</u> when building a following

- You must <u>be active</u> in social media to build and maintain your online image

SOCIAL MEDIA GOALS

Social media has many qualities that, when harnessed, can absolutely propel your business exponentially. Social media marketing can help with goals like:

- Increasing website traffic

- Building conversions

- Raising brand awareness

- Creating an identity & positive brand association

- Improving communication and interaction with a key audience

Small businesses can implement social media strategies to reach and engage existing and potential clients, while spreading the word about their products and services.

In today's connected world, where customers research purchases online and seek recommendations from friends and family, it is in the best interest of the smallest businesses to have a vibrant and interactive social media presence.

SAVINGS SECRET #16   EDUCATION &
TRAINING AS TAX DEDUCTIONS

This includes seminars, but don't forget any workshops that are related to your business or industry. They are all 100 percent tax deductible.

What's in the next chapter?

It all begins to come together with a business plan. ▶

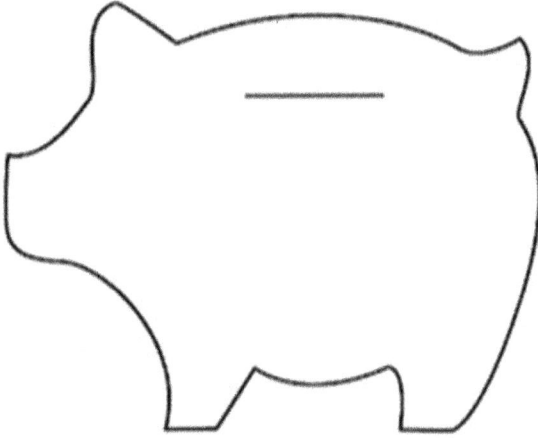

CHAPTER SEVEN:

CREATING A BUSINESS PLAN

A carefully considered business plan helps business owners focus on strategic objectives on the pathway to success.

CHAPTER SEVEN:

CREATING A BUSINESS PLAN

A business plan is an extremely important tool that every business owner should create and have readily available to review on a regular basis. A review must occur either quarterly or at least semi-annually. A business plan does not just serve as a litmus test to determine the viability and the feasibility of your business. It is a guide, a road map to take you from your present position to the level you desire to attain. A carefully considered plan helps business owners focus on strategic objectives on the path to success.

If you are considering a business loan, most lending companies will require a copy of a business plan. A business plan is a prerequisite for you to succeed in your networking, home-based business, franchise or really any business you desire. You have so much to gain by creating a solid business plan, so make sure you do not take any short cuts, but put in the necessary time to create a solid plan. A well-written business plan will play a key role in the success of your business.

The challenges facing a start-up are very clear. You must learn your business, establish and expand your customer base, and develop a business strategy. During this initial stage, you should prepare a business plan, determine the structure of your business, and begin to think about investment management and tax management (more on tax advantages later). Planning is essential, but you must also call on customers and do everything that you can to generate cash. *DO NOT PROCRASTINATE! TIME IS $$$!*

<u>SAVINGS SECRET #17</u>   **TAX DEDUCTION FOR INSURANCE PREMIUMS**

You can deduct premiums that you pay for credit, liability, malpractice and workers' compensation insurance among others.

If you are in the planning stages of starting your first venture, a good business plan will help you to:

- Change what are your thoughts and ideas into a profitable business

- question the validity of your ideas, products or services

- Get the needed start-up financing from potential investors and lenders

- Develop business alliances

- Identify the following:

  - the strengths of your business

  - the feasible weaknesses that are not readily apparent

  - opportunities a new or existing business may present

  - the potential internal and external threats to the business

  - what resources, other than financial, that may be required

If you are already a business owner, your goal should be to become a more established firm or entity in the marketplace. Indeed, you may want to become the preferred company in your industry, but it is still important to maintain a cash reserve, watch expenses and guard against unforeseen problems.

Although a company can always use more cash, most growing firms will get by on their own limited resources. The business owner should understand his or her business at this point, as well as the key competitors. If you are already a business owner, a good business plan can assist you in:

- Communicating your vision effectively to employees and any interested parties

- Developing a reliable financial forecast

- Looking toward expansion and attracting and retaining key employees
- Making comparison between your proposed and actual performance
- Helping a business stay organized and on track

When businesses crack the local market and manage their affairs efficiently, they become more mature. Mature firms, commonly have achieved a certain amount of name recognition, at least on a local level. Contacts are generally well-established, the business produces a reliable stream of cash, and borrowing for growth or to purchase assets becomes easier.

At this point in the maturity of your business, perhaps intensive marketing may be needed to increase or maintain market position, but product innovation may not be a factor. Profit margins tend to stabilize as a business matures, unless the business is seasonal in nature.

Nevertheless, for a mature enterprise, a good business plan is extremely vital in:

- Creating good strategies for effectively managing business growth
- Raising capital for business expansion
- Taking advantage of opportunities and lowering risks

- Adapting to a changing marketplace environment
- Staying competitive and in some cases will become more innovative
- Scrutinizing expenses
- Analyzing and updating a business's valuation

SAVINGS SECRET #19   **TAX DEDUCTIONS FOR FURNITURE**

You can either deduct the entire cost in the year of the purchase or depreciate it over several years.

What are my business goals?

The first step in planning is to set the goals and objectives for your business. The goals should be such that they will contribute meaningfully to the short-term, as well as, long-term business visions. Your goals must not be ambiguous; they should be clearly stated and understandable. Another detail that's very important when setting goals, is formulating them in a POSITIVE manner. Remember that what you focus on, increases.

Your business goals must pass the **SMART** examination if they are to be effective. What that means is that the goals you set forth for your business, must be <u>S</u>pecific, <u>M</u>easurable, <u>A</u>chievable, <u>R</u>ealistic and <u>T</u>imely. When your goals have these attributes, they provide clarity to your business pursuits and you will be able to evaluate your business's performance against these goals and have a confident feeling about the results. **SMART** goals will greatly enhance your chances to succeed.

SMART GOALS

SMART goal-setting follows a tested process developed over many years by countless companies around the world. I worked for a company in the 1980's that used a form of **SMART** goal procedures. Once pushed through the **SMART** system, the goals become extremely effective. In order for goals to become or qualify as **SMART**, they must be:

SPECIFIC: Your goals must be _**specific**_, not broad or wide-ranging. When you have specific goals, it will usually guarantee a better understanding of what the intent of the goal is. There will not be any misunderstandings or misinterpretations.

MEASURABLE: SMART goals must be ***measurable*** and this can be accomplished in monetary, distance, weight or many other figures and terms. In order to be measureable, you need to have established criteria to measure the progress made against the set goals.

The key word is "measureable". Let's have some fun for a moment; let's say for example, a golfer like me, who does not generally have time for a round of golf, might set a goal of just enjoying the good weather, good friends and having a wonderful time away from the office. For me, this would be a fantastic goal, but it is subjective and not measurable.

For a golf enthusiast, a measurable goal would be to score less than an 80 for the 18-hole round and no single-hole score greater than a 6. Just for good measure, maybe we add that the golfer cannot hit or lose any golf balls in the water. This does not sound like much fun on the course if this goal was set for me! The point is, the goal set for the golf enthusiast is certainly a measurable one, and would qualify as a **SMART** goal.

**SAVINGS SECRET #18   STARTUP EXPENSES
(capital) TAX DEDUCTIONS**

You can choose to deduct up to $5,000 of startup costs, which include any research costs incurred for creating your business.

ACHIEVABLE: The achievable goals should stretch yourself or your workers, but not break them. While goals can be ambitious, they should always be ***achievable***. This is where common sense or reality has to play a part in goal-setting.

When you are overly ambitious in setting goals and they become unachievable, in most cases it will demoralize you or an employee. Set up ambitious and yet achievable goals which will truly inspire you to fully utilize your talents, as well as, making good use of every opportunity at your disposal to achieve the goals.

I learned a lesson many years ago when I sensed one of my sales representatives was "dogging" it and not putting forth the effort to close on sales at an appropriate level for the geographic area. So, I set the goals for the following year at a level high enough to make up for my "perceived" low sales level from the previous year.

The consequence of my action was that the salesperson ended up leaving the company. I never made that mistake again. I learned that I was not "in touch" with reality. My sales expectations where not based in what was achievable. What I mean is, achievable under normal circumstances in that particular marketplace.

RELEVANT: Are your goals going to help your business grow? Are these worthwhile goals? Your business goals should be in line with the mission of your business and of interest to your customers. The goals you set must be **_relevant_** to your business. In other words, do the goals reflect the long-term objectives? As your business and products change, your goals should reflect those changes. Last but certainly not least, are there enough monetary resources to achieve the goals?

TIMELY: Each of your goals should have a reasonable time frame for completion. Are the goals **_timely_**? Give yourself enough time to achieve your goals, but don't set your deadline so far in advance that you lose motivation. Be realistic when deciding how much time it will take to gain 25 new customers, for example.

In order to become effective, having time-bound objectives serves as a motivating factor to get the goals achieved within the specified time frame. For instance, you can have targets for every quarter of the year.

Further, by setting SMART goals and objectives, they will become measurable and **DO NOT FORGET**, following up on their completion is paramount.

KEY POINT: you have to be determined and focus on achieving your goals, so as to avoid discouragement and distraction. It is suggested that you should review your goals periodically (at least semi-annually) to ensure you are on course.

Having set your goals, you need to map out strategies to achieve the goals. As a business owner for example, your strategy could be to introduce innovations, more marketing and networking.

Reviewing the compensation plan

Just a few words about compensation plans. Most businesses and organizations usually find it difficult to have a suitable compensation and benefits policy. But it is even more difficult to have an appropriate compensation plan in a business that is just taking off. Therefore, you need to strike a good balance. So how do you go about setting up the compensation plan?

First, you need to have a realistic understanding about the limitations of your new business. For a business that has spent less than a year in the marketplace, there is no way to match the benefits and salaries offered by more established competitors.

On the other hand, there are certain advantages to be derived from being a small or new startup entity. Since you have no fixed and permanent compensation plans, you can tailor your compensation and benefits to your specific needs. You need to be creative and flexible to achieve this.

Secondly, you have to be comprehensive and logical in analyzing the options available to you. It can be quite expensive to design, install, manage and terminate compensation and benefit plans. If your compensation plan is badly or inappropriately conceived, the plan can eventually become a costly mistake.

As a business owner, you need to make an evaluation of your compensation and benefit plans and the alternatives available to you from four different perspectives.

How do they affect cash flow?

As a new or start up business, **survival is your number one priority**, not cash compensation. Nonetheless, you must continue to strive to attract the best talent into your business even with your restricted spending ability. It may take a while, so just figure you will be working longer hours and have less "free" time on your hands. **Remember:** survival is your number one priority for a new or startup business.

SAVINGS SECRET #20   TAX DEDUCTIONS FOR TELEPHONE & INTERNET

You can deduct the cost of business calls that you make for business from home. When your bill comes in, circle the business-related calls, total them up and keep a copy. At the end of the year, tally your 12 bills and deduct 100 percent. The IRS warns that regular fees and charges don't count toward your deduction.

What are the tax implications?

Your choice of compensation and benefit plans comes with varying tax consequences. For a business that is just starting up, you can make use of the 72,000-page tax code to derive the maximum gain in your compensation choices or make it easier for yourself, consult with a tax expert. The laws are changing each and every year. Do yourself a favor, check with a Certified Public Accountant or a tax attorney.

What is the accounting impact?

As a business owner, you need to know that different compensation plans also have different ways of affecting your income statement. **I REPEAT**: make it easier for yourself, make sure to consult with a tax expert. The laws are changing each and every year. Do yourself a favor, check with a Certified Public Accountant or a tax attorney.

What is the competition doing?

No business operates in isolation. Even more importantly, when the business is striving to recruit talented people onto the team, you need to consider the trends and customs of your industry before finalizing any compensation plans.

As a startup business, when it comes to making a decision on compensation policies, you have to make some difficult and tough choices. When your business starts experiencing growth and financial stability, you will have the temptation to enhance your compensation plans. Do your best not to give in to those temptations. Over time, your business will become more mature and you will have a better compensation plan. Take a slow incremental approach to a final compensation plan.

Lastly, remember there are taxes to pay, cash flow implications, as well as, accounting considerations as a consequence of any choice you make.

Is there any funding required?

The most crucial element of any business startup is funding. There are many essential items which may require funding like: office space, development of your brand, product or marketing and promotions. Funding may be needed to make your presence felt online. It is safe to say, adequate funding is generally necessary for the overall success of the business.

> ## <u>SAVINGS SECRET #21</u>   TAX DEDUCTION FOR WEBSITE DESIGN/HOSTING
>
> Yes, all website design, implementation and hosting are fully-deductible as a tax deduction.

There are many sources through which you can get your business funded. Some of the more popular means available for securing funding for your business are discussed below:

Sources of Funds for Business Start Ups

1. Own money

Most new business owners usually prefer starting their business with their savings. Although for those with insufficient savings, there are other alternative sources of funding that can explored, such as:

- Borrowing privately
- Getting a mortgage
- Selling off possessions or assets
- Acquiring a loan

With self-financing, you have greater control of your business which is quite a bit more than any other financing sources.

2. Borrow from banks or lending institutions

Obtaining loans and overdrafts from local banks and credit unions is a very popular source of business financing. However, a bank will usually determine if you are credit worthy before lending or funding your business. If you are a new or startup business, or the business does not have any resources yet, you will probably be asked for collateral in the form of hard assets, like personal real estate property, insurance policies and much more.

In order to determine your credit worthiness, a bank may require you to submit at least the following:

- A good business plan
- Evidence of having a successful business track record
- Security or collateral for the intended loan

3. Family and friends

Let's assume you did not succeed in raising sufficient capital from the lending institutions or your savings; you can also approach your family and friends for assistance. The beauty about sourcing funds from your family and friends is that most of the time, you will receive an interest-free loan from them. It is advisable to mark down the terms any time there is an exchange of family money involved. It is protection for both you and your family member.

4. Attract outside investors

Quite often, when you receive funding from external investors, they may not only provide you with the necessary funding, they may possibly provide you with expertise in your industry or line of business. In this case, unlike overdrafts and loans, you are generally under no obligation to pay back the money until you have the ability to pay.

Furthermore, getting extra funding from the investors will improve your credit worthiness with the banks should the need arise at a later date.

ON THE OTHER SIDE OF THE COIN: If there are external investors in your business, they could demand a high return, though not necessarily in cash but a piece or portion of your business. A return on an external investor's outlay could be in the form of high loan interest or shares in the business. **Warning:** funds from external investors can become a very risky proposition for a variety of reasons, so consult with an attorney who specializes in contract law.

5. Grants and government support

If you happen to own or want to start a business, there may be government grant or loan options available to you. The great aspect of government-funded loans is often the interest terms are very favorable for the business owner. If you are willing to do some leg work and visit some of the government agencies offering low-interest loans, you may be surprised to learn what funding may be available. Check with your local librarian as a library is loaded with government periodicals offering details about loans and grants. Also, The U.S. Small Business Administration (SBA) has an entire website dedicated to grants and loans for small businesses. These are two great resources at your disposal.

What's in the next chapter?

It is said that great people make a great company. ▶

CHAPTER EIGHT:

TEAM BUILDING

The greatest business owners, and the people who have built successful companies, may not be the smartest. They are people who have harnessed the talents of their team to build great businesses.

CHAPTER EIGHT:

TEAM BUILDING

It is said that great people make a great company, and as a business owner, your main goal is to form the business into a huge success. Well, to make that dream a reality, a lot depends on your team or employees. A business is only successful because of the great team behind it.

I firmly believe this concept due to my personal true-life experience. I once had a managerial position with a large international firm in the late 80's. As a product manager, I worked with over 70 sales representatives in 12 states at a time when the Internet was just becoming widely used. At the time, I conducted many "live" training sessions because there was no such training or communication tool like a webinar.

The point to be made here is that through employee training and providing the tools they needed to succeed, meant I did not have to constantly travel and be away from my wife and kids. I called it the "Train-the-Trainer" Program. Due to the select small group of wonderful people taking the lead and training the entry-level positioned people, meant I only had to travel on a limited basis once the program was in motion. You can be very talented and come up with the business idea of the century or invent the greatest product ever known to man or you can have an amazing brand name; but, if you do not have the correct people to take charge of the business, the odds are that it will never reach the full potential or may possibly fail.

The roles of your team members and other employees in ensuring that your business achieves success is so very important. That is why you need to have good people on your team and when they have become part of the team, _**you** have a duty to make it known that they are an integral part of the business._

A top-quality business owner is not necessarily someone who has all the skills and talents to solely carry out all that is needed to create a successful business. As a matter of fact, most business owners who believe that they alone are the building blocks of their businesses and underrate the skills and talents of their employees or team members, usually end up being just a self-employed business owner.

On the other hand, good business men and women understand that they need people who are better, smarter, and more skillful to build a great business. They truly understand that they only need to harness the talents of their team and watch them produce amazing results.

In fact, the greatest business owners and the people who have built successful companies may not be the smartest.

They are people who have harnessed the talents of their team to build great businesses.

SAVINGS SECRET #22   PROFESSIONAL
PUBLICATIONS DEDUCTION

This includes any magazines, books, CDs and DVDs that are related to your business or industry. They are all 100 percent tax deductible.

In order to build a winning team for your business, it is strongly suggested that you take the following steps:

1. You must identify the right people for your business. What type of person do you perceive is going to help you build your business? Don't gloss over this step. The more time you spend on identifying the right people, the better off you will be in the long run. Once you have identified the type of person your business needs, go to the next step.

2. You need to find and attract these people. Since you have identified the type of person you need to grow your business, the next step is to ascertain or determine where these people are located. In this step you may elect to use the Internet; Facebook and LinkedIn are great social media tools you can use for this phase. If you are more of a traditionalist, then

newspapers, local magazines and flyers to run classified-type ads may be more to your liking. I would submit that the Internet will yield better results and less expensive in the long run.

3. You need to select and qualify these people based on their skills, abilities and talents. In this step, you are the interviewer. If you lack the confidence to perform this step, there are many resources that can be used to create good quality interview questions and assemble an easy-to-follow outline.

4. If you don't have a mission or vision statement, create one or both and then make sure your new team player understands and internalizes them.

5. Continue to work with them through the early stages so this person gets to understand what your expectations are. The more time spent in these early formative days and weeks will create a better working relationship and will bring out the best in your team player.

SAVINGS SECRET #23   **TAX DEDUCTION FOR ASSOCIATION DUES/FEES**

Association dues and associated fees are generally tax deductible when related to your existing business.

WHAT ARE THE QUALITIES OF A TEAM MEMBER?

In selecting the right people for your team, you need to consider some important qualities. Although some human assets may not be readily noticeable during the 1st interview, a 2nd or even a 3rd interview is always an appropriate action to take. If your current team has good "chemistry", you certainly do not want to upset the harmony. Consider the following:

- **Demonstrates reliability**

Your team member must be someone who will be reliable. This person should be an individual who will get the job done within the time schedule; must be hardworking and someone who will follow through any given assignment. This must be someone you can always rely on to perform with or without any pressure, or more importantly, a person you do not need to "babysit".

- **Constructive Communicators**

For a team to function effectively, they need individuals who will express their minds openly and who will state their ideas clearly and honestly as it concerns the work of the team.

- **Functions as an active participant**

A good team member should be able to participate actively to promote the work of the team. Further, there has to be a sense of equity and fairness among the team members.

- **Honest and Straightforward**

This is a very important quality needed in a good team member; you don't need people who will play games with you. You need honest people who will be able to tell you anything good or bad for the greater good of the business.

★ **Bonus Business Tip:**
For meals & entertainment deductions, document at least the following on each receipt:
WHO, WHAT, WHY, WHERE, WHEN & HOW MUCH

- **Complements Others' Skills**

For the team to be effective, it is very important that the team members are able to complement one another. Keep in mind, that people have different areas of strengths and weaknesses. An important characteristic of an effective work team is what is often called, "the shared capacity". The team member must have some special skills to contribute to the progress of the team, or moving the team in a forward motion.

- **Positive Attitude**

A positive mentality is very important to the overall success of the team. A team member must have a positive attitude, a "can do" spirit. Think about it, no one would ever follow a negative or cynical leader.

THIS ONE IS FOR YOU -- NETWORK MARKETER OR A HOME-BASED BUSINESS

- **Building Downlines**

Downlines, or legs, are people you recruit to join in your business opportunity and it is a very common practice in multi-level marketing, although other types of businesses can also gain from this practice. When you are building downlines, you must remember that everyone is helping one another to achieve the desired success – the goal, the prize, *the money*. By building a strong downline, you will have countless benefits in the future including building of residual or passive income.

Ensure that you recruit the right people into your networking or home-based business, because when you make the mistake of bringing in people that have no business training, they will be unable to recruit other people into the business. If you goal is building a team, then recruit properly.

Who has had a bad experience with network marketing?

I have been in several network marketing groups over the past 45 years, so I have the experience. In the early days, I only had a list of friends and family that would buy products. I did not have the right people to build a business. I had the wrong mindset. I was "selling" my contacts on products, not building a business. Every presentation I have ever attended, (and there have been many) the main lecturer spoke about the great products and how much money they made. That's good to hear, but I never heard one person ever speak about building the business by bringing in the right people **AND** giving them the tools to succeed. I only heard them say, "go forth and make a list of people you know and invite them to your home for a presentation." A home party is not for me.

No wonder network marketing received a "black eye" in the late 70's and early 80's. I was never educated about bringing in the right people and giving them the tools to succeed. The "tools" are training videos, books, documents, brochures, etc. I am not saying that you can't have customers who buy products; what I am saying is that if you are going to build a business and increase your residual income, you can't afford to bring unproductive people into the business or organization.

Recruiting people can be costly and it is certainly time consuming; therefore, _you need to spend your resources on people that will produce good results_.

SAVINGS SECRET #24   CONVENTIONS & TRADE SHOWS DEDUCTION

This includes existing business-related trade shows. They are all 100 percent tax deductible.

There is a need for you to target your recruitment efforts to those who will be interested in what you have to offer and also have interest in marketing your product, service or the business themselves.

First and foremost, you must look in the "mirror". Effective leaders periodically take stock of their personal strengths and shortcomings. They ask: "What do I like to do? What am I really good at?" "What are my areas of weakness, and what do I dislike doing?" You have to be honest with yourself.

Knowing your areas of weakness does not make you weak; on the contrary, it allows you to delegate to others who have those abilities, in order to achieve the common goal. Rather than clinging to the false belief that they can do it all, great leaders hire people who complement, rather than supplement, their skills. Working on your areas of weaknesses will improve your leadership ability – and recognizing them makes you more human.

With the introduction of internet marketing into the recruiting process or system, the problem of building downlines has been drastically reduced. With the Internet, you can easily target and locate other people that will have an interest in the business, service or product you are promoting.

After locating those interested in your products, you only need to give them an offer that reasonably supersedes that of the competition and they will gladly join up with you.

In addition, you can also show your downline how you are carrying out your own recruitment process. Since your recruits are rightly targeted, they will have interest in knowing how you successfully carry out or utilize your effective recruiting system. It is then and only then, will they go ahead and replicate your strategy.

Following through with this process you will be able to build an effective downline for your home-based or network marketing business.

Much more will be written in my next book specifically targeting network marketing and home-based businesses.

What's in the next chapter?

BEWARE of the roadblocks. ▶

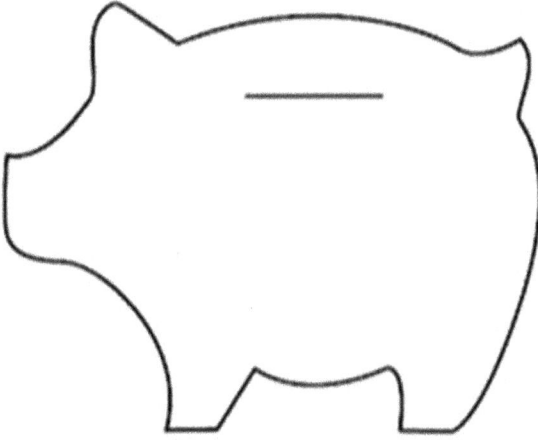

CHAPTER NINE:

BEWARE OF ROADBLOCKS

Owning a business can be a family decision. If married, and even before the search begins, the family needs honest discussions about the benefits and challenges of a business

CHAPTER NINE:

BEWARE OF ROADBLOCKS

Many people who dream of independence, who have amazing business ideas with the potential to become the next big thing in the business world, have had their dreams shattered before they ever get started. Others, started out with high levels of enthusiasm, and still others had a passion and that awesome entrepreneurial spirit in their heart and soul.

Nevertheless, their journey down Entrepreneur Lane was short-lived because of their failure to recognize and subsequently failed to create a strategy or a way of overcoming the obstacles blocking their progress. Many potential entrepreneurs have failed to recognize these common obstacles or impediments because roadblocks can be commonplace and a part of the day-to-day life. That's why they never suspect them to be a hindrance.

Handling these roadblocks beforehand can improve your odds for success. So what are road blocks that could prevent an entrepreneur from fulfilling the "burning desire" to becoming a successful business owner?

Spousal roadblock

This type of obstacle is not uncommon among married entrepreneurs. The discussion of your business idea with your spouse might raise some concern or even outright objections from them because they see things from a different perspective.

If you are not careful, the disagreement over your business idea has the potential to create a marital problem. The failure of your partner to recognize the potential of the business the same way you perceived it, could be discouraging for you. A spousal roadblock often leads to lost enthusiasm to start a business. Who knows, the idea for a business venture may have become a great success had it not been for the roadblock.

SAVINGS SECRET #25   FREIGHT / SHIPPING COSTS TAX DEDUCTION

This includes existing business-related freight and shipping costs. 100 percent tax deductible.

How to overcome a spousal roadblock

1. As a married man/woman, you need to understand that the decision to own a business should be made by the couples, and are "in concert" with one another about the decision. The discussion about becoming a business owner must occur between both parties. The couple needs honest discussions about the benefits and challenges of business ownership.

   Owning a business is a family decision. Even before the search begins, the couple needs honest discussions about the benefits and challenges of business ownership.

2. In my opinion, if there is a spousal roadblock to becoming a business owner, then you have to make sure you have stated or presented your case with all the facts. Investing in a business is one of the most important decisions to be made and calls for full agreement from both partners.

   Prior to raising the idea about a new business and discussing with my wife, I created a pros & cons list without fail. I know it sounds like I am over simplifying the process, but I look at it this way, if I can work through all the potential negative issues prior to a discussion with my wife, then I have a better chance of furthering my idea to start a business.

After all, if I can't get through all the cons by myself, maybe I am promoting the wrong business!

3. Make sure it is understood with your spouse -- as a business owner, you will likely have to work long hours and may have fewer opportunities to take off for personal time, especially extended vacations. Also, and this is a big one, the income from a new business may not be steady AND there may be times when there is very little or no income at all.

4. If both spouses are in agreement and want to own a business, or get involved in a business, it is important that both attend any meeting that relates to the business. Why is this important? Both of you must have the same information.

    Making investments, especially starting, owning and running a business, is a very important decision that requires the agreement of you and your spouse. Would you want your spouse to buy a house, or maybe a car, or changing jobs without your input?

SAVINGS SECRET #26   **TAX DEDUCTION FOR POSTAGE**

This includes existing business-related postage costs - 100 percent tax deductible.

The friend/ neighbor roadblock

While it is flattering to be asked for their opinion, your friends and neighbors constitute another stumbling block you need to be cautious of. When you inform them of your proposed business idea or plan, you must keep in mind that friends and neighbors will cheerfully provide their "uninformed" opinions about your business opportunity.

Remember, your friends and neighbors will not have the same interests and knowledge about your business choice, nor will they have completed the amount of research that you will have performed up to this point. They will feed off of your excitement, and in most cases they will express opinions they perceive you desire to hear. Give each opinion offered by friends the time for discussion based on the knowledge and business experience of the opinion giver.

The way out

The opinions of your neighbors shouldn't be the sole basis for making a decision. Go ahead and note their comments on your pros & cons list. Since you asked their opinion, you will need to consider their point of view but only give it enough weight based on the expertise and the business knowledge of the person offering such opinion.

The self and Internet roadblock

Most people are the architects of their business failures by mixing up real research with a casual inquiry.

For instance, you may be interested in a business and proceed to do a casual check on multiple Internet search engines. You get some information to use as a basis for making business decisions, but in most cases your data will not have important information about market size, the available niches or even the primary targets of the business. Also, be careful to note how current and up-to-date the information is.

Your mindset can be the biggest obstacle to overcome in your business. Many people carry around a false belief about themselves that needs to be removed or improved. In business, you are the gateway to your company.

The only way to conquer a self-limiting belief is by recognizing a negative mindset and taking action to overcome it. Time and persistence can overcome such shortcomings.

The way out

You can get quality information and opinions from those who are into the business already; so don't be afraid to ask questions of other business owners. Also, many counties across the country have government-funded programs to assist current and potential business owners. Have you checked with any of your state colleges or universities for small business development centers which typically offer workshops, training and business counseling at a reduced cost?

Why not give your dreams a fighting chance? When you make assumptions, you give away your power to fears and concerns that may not even turn out to be valid. I'm always amazed at how "insurmountable" dreams can turn into reality with a little faith, research and effort to make the proper decision.

I can't stress this enough, "when performing research about a business or industry, be serious about it." This may be the most important decision you will ever make in your entire life. Why not be as informed as possible?

What's in the next chapter?

Advantages of a home-based business. ▶

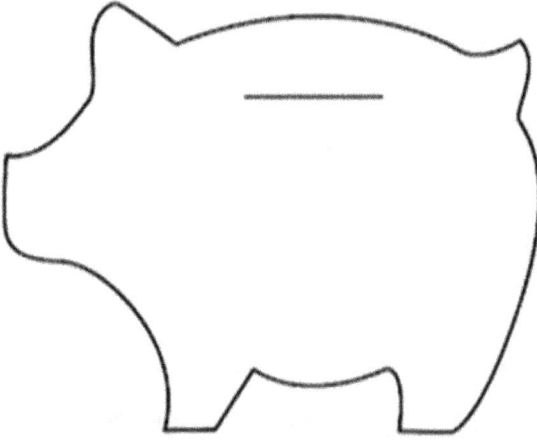

CHAPTER TEN:

ADVANTAGES OF A HOME-BASED BUSINESS

Although working at home requires self-discipline, the benefits can be substantial - especially in the start-up years.

CHAPTER TEN:

ADVANTAGES OF A NETWORK MARKETING OR HOME BASED BUSINESS

Although I am at work on another book devoted to network marketing and home-based businesses, I wanted to write a few words about the developing opportunities in this industry. Home-based businesses are quickly becoming the fastest growing form of business startups. Developing your company out of your home allows for flexibility that is difficult when renting or buying office and warehouse space. Although working at home requires self-discipline, the benefits can be substantial - especially in the start-up years.

If you are tired of waking up every morning and dragging yourself to a place of employment you don't really take pleasure in, just so that you can make ends meet, starting a home-based business or network marketing is probably the best decision that you would ever make.

With the increasing rate at which companies downsize their workforce, it becomes even more lucrative to start or run (manage) a home-based business. If you have ever had the desire to be in control of your time, take charge of your future, get out of the rat race and have quality time to spend with your family, then a home-based business has the potential to make your dream a reality. Other benefits of network marketing or a home-based business include:

1. **Personal freedom**: A home-based business affords the opportunity to become your own boss; there is generally no need to travel to an office or jobsite; you decide what you do with your time; you have more peace of mind because you no longer have to deal with an unhappy boss or unpleasant office politics. All that is required is your passion, the discipline and ability to make judicious use of your time and to have that entrepreneurial spirt in your soul.

2. **You get to keep the money you make:** You are not working hard or long hours for anybody but yourself and family. Most generally, your income depends on how hardworking you are, or in some circles, the efficient use of your time may translate into more income. The money earned is all yours and you can achieve financial independence through many home based-business opportunities. You have limitless opportunities to do what you like.

3. **Less risky:** You don't need to break the bank to start a home-business. In most cases, it requires less capital as compared to a traditional business.

4. **Tax advantages:** You benefit from many tax advantages since you have your office located in your home. Check out chapter 11.

5. **Time:** You have more time to spend with your family and friends.

6. **Low stress:** Running a home-based business is generally not too stressful, and you can conveniently combine your business and family demands.

7. **Personal growth:** Since you are now the boss, you can experience personal growth because you become many things at once, the CEO, director, sales manager, etc. As time marches on, all these roles will enhance your skills and assist in making you a better-equipped individual to continue building your successful business.

SAVINGS SECRET #27   DEDUCTIONS FOR PARKING & TOLLS

If you drive for business, the IRS allows for parking and tolls when paid for an existing business. The IRS loves documentation, so keep a notebook in your vehicle to record the date, mileage, tolls, parking costs and the purpose of your trip.

What's in the next chapter?

27 tax-savings secrets your business can't survive without. ▶

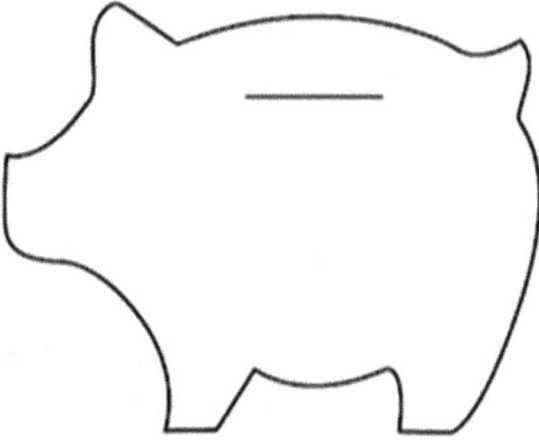

CHAPTER ELEVEN:

27 TAX-SAVING SECRETS YOUR BUSINESS CAN'T SURVIVE WITHOUT

Believe it or not, the IRS Tax Code is written in part to help businesses grow and prosper. Listed in this chapter are 27 of the most common deductions to help increase your profits!

CHAPTER ELEVEN:

Tax-Saving Secrets Your Business Can't Survive Without

Living in the United States is expensive -- from paying our share of taxes to the federal, state and local governments, business expenses and our own personal expenses. It sure seems like everywhere I go, I am constantly reaching for my billfold.

It is a well-published fact that there are many millions of small businesses in America. Recently, I read an article claiming that some 53% of small business owners were not taking advantage of or claiming tax deductions available to them. This was according to some government statistics and I was astonished by this fact!

As an owner of several small businesses over the past 40 years, one of the best decisions I had ever made was finding a good CPA (he later became a great personal friend of mine) who was constantly teaching me to think above the line – the Adjusted Gross Income line.

What is meant by thinking above this line is constantly trying to determine which expenses may have a business purpose. For me, this thought process became so ingrained that it is almost impossible for me to purchase something without first considering a tax benefit or purpose for that item or service.

Hint: any business owner must become proficient at keeping good records and realizing when expenses have a legitimate business purpose.

Myth: Taking less deductions will decrease the chance of an IRS audit.

NOTE: Of course, as with any article, brochure or book you may read, tax-savings tips should never take the place of expert advice from a tax accountant, lawyer or CPA.

All tax-saving tips listed here are for U.S. based businesses only. If your company resides outside of the United States, please check with your tax advisor about what comparable tips apply in your specific country.

There are some basic and yet effective tips you can employ to file your taxes; however, always act in accordance with the advice presented by your tax advisor to make sure you are taking every legal deduction you are entitled to.

Here are 27 tax-saving tips that even savvy small-business owners and entrepreneurs sometimes forget when preparing tax returns:

27 Tax-Saving Secrets For Small & Home-Based Businesses	
Home Office - Home office must be dedicated to your business	15 **Charitable Contributions** - see IRS Publication 561 to determine eligibility
Advertising & Marketing - Must be directly related to your business	16 **Education & Training** - Seminars, workshops, continuing education
Depreciation - Property purchased to use in your business	17 **Insurance Premiums** - Premiums for credit, liability, malpractice & others
Auto Maintenance - Two methods to calculate vehicle deductions	18 **Startup Expenses (capital expenses)** - May choose up to $5,000 in deductions
Auto Mileage - Two methods to calculate vehicle deductions	19 **Furniture** - Office furniture is deductible in 1 or more years
Utilities - 100% deductible for office / Must split out personal	20 **Telephone & Internet** - Any dedicated business use (less personal use)
Property Repairs - Business only repairs	21 **Website Design & Hosting** - 100% Business deduction (no for personal use)
Property Maintenance - Business only property maintenance	22 **Professional Publications** - Books, CDs, DVDs, magazines (business-related)
Licenses - License, as well as regulatory fees, are deductible	23 **Association Dues & Fees** - All professional dues (if related to your business)
Office Supplies - Pens, paper, staples, ink, etc.	24 **Conventions & Trade Shows** - Business-related expenses only (no personal)
Professional Fees - Accountant, attorney, consulting fees are deductible	25 **Freight & Shipping Costs** - When costs are associated to business functions
Travel Expenses - Business-related airfare, hotels, taxi, meals	26 **Postage** - Business use only
Interest - Business mortgage, finance charges, some interest	27 **Parking & Tolls** - Business use only (note reason for expense)
Software - Boxed or downloaded software are deductible	The Business Owner's Savings Bible

- **Good record keeping is key in successfully claiming all the business deductions to which you are entitled to.**

- **Verify everything with copies of bills, invoices, paystubs, mileage logs for vehicles, etc.**

- **A complete read through of the IRS small business publications is well worth the time.**

IRS

Department of the Treasury

- **Publication 334 (2015), Tax Guide for Small Business**
- **Small Business and Self-Employed Tax Center serves taxpayers who file Form 1040, Schedules C, E, F or Form 2106, as well as small businesses with assets under $10 million.**

Most small business deductions are a bit more complicated than can be explained in this brief overview, but this is a good introduction to the basics.

Remember, any item you're not sure whether a purchase is a legitimate business expense, ask yourself, "Is this an ordinary and necessary expense in my line of work?" This is the same question the IRS will ask when examining your expenses if you get audited. If the answer is no, don't take the deduction.

If you're not sure, seek professional help with your tax return from a CPA or tax attorney.

BONUS BUSINESS TIPS

▶ Deductions create cash that you never have to pay back!

▶ For every 100 business miles driven at $0.54 per mile (IRS for year 2016) = $54.00 for an auto mileage tax deduction. At a 33% tax bracket = $17.82 cash savings. (using the IRS Mileage Rate Method)

▶ Meals & Entertainment deductions are possible if:

#1. You are running your business like a business (you may need to offer proof if you are ever called in for an audit)

#2. The reason for claiming this deduction is the promotion of business in pursuit of a profit. (you do not have to close a sale, just the pursuit of the sale)

► Deduct up to 50% of an entertainment expense if you talk business in the same 24-hour day
  (i.e. lunch and then a baseball game)

► With a home office deduction, you may qualify to claim a portion of: utilities, home interest, taxes, depreciation, security service, cleaning service, rent plus much more.

► For meals & entertainment deductions, it is <u>recommended that you document</u>:

WHO – was in attendance?
WHAT – was discussed?
WHY – was this meeting important?
WHERE – did the meeting take place?
WHEN – did the meeting take place?
HOW MUCH – was the expense?

FINAL THOUGHTS

Your dream for true financial freedom can <u>never</u> be realized if you still depend on an employer to provide a job so you can work for your income. No one but you - can make a decision to start your own small business. No corporate organization provides real financial security and the present situation of economies all over the world has made job security almost like a mirage. It is very nearly a matter of necessity that you start your own business – right now!

Many entrepreneurs consider themselves "Type-A" personalities, folks that like to take control and make decisions. It is just like saying, "Owning a business saves them from having to work for anyone else." For a small business owner, you are able to make your own decisions about how best to operate on a day-to-day basis and this leads to creating a culture, a brand and an organization.

One of the most of-cited benefits of owning your own business is the flexibility that comes with it; whether that would be working from wherever you want or setting your own hours for a non-brick and mortar business. Just as important, entrepreneurs say that owning their own business allows them to set their own personal priorities.

When you work for someone else, you rarely get to choose whom you work with. If you don't like your co-workers, you better start sending out resumes. That's not the case when you own your own business, since you get to make the decisions about who to hire, should you decide to expand.

Surround yourself with positive people who give you the confidence and optimism you need to keep moving forward. The smaller your organization, the greater choice you have about who you work with.

There is no question that owning your own business can be a risky proposition. I've heard many times, with risk comes reward. In other words, the better you are at managing risk, the more future rewards you are able to reap. Every day is filled with new challenges, and in the first few years, there are generally more challenges faced by new business owners. While you must live with the consequences from the decisions that were made (good or bad), every day will be a learning experience.

There is great satisfaction when you have worked several years and overcoming many of the obstacles to create a business you can be proud to call your own. You can also be proud of the fact that your customers enjoy your products or services. There is a sense of enormous pride in establishing and building a new or established business of your own.

Many entrepreneurs love the idea that in building their business, they can give back to the community whether through job creation or donation of products or services. There is something very special about helping others.

Good, solid, serious research and surrounding yourself with good friends and family will lead you to the best decision. Talk to the successful business owners. When you have gathered the information and are honest about your own abilities, you will make a smart, educated decision for you, your family and your future.

To your success.

Ed Klaameyer

WHAT READERS ARE SAYING ABOUT THIS BOOK

"The Business Owner's Savings Bible is a MUST READ for anyone who is desiring to start their own business OR is currently operating a small business. It is a practical, step-by-step manual for the emerging small business owner. The author, Ed Klaameyer, takes the reader through a series of relevant questions, considerations, business tips and tax savings advice that will help ensure and increase the business owner's ROI – return on investment. I highly recommend this quick read, and in-depth tool." - GABY HARRIS, LegalShield, www.tgharris.net, Trinity, FL

"As a barber pursuing my dream. I appreciate the author's focus on choosing a career that best suits you. You will learn how important it is to be doing something you love! The information on tax deductions were most beneficial to me." - JOSHUA, Joshua the Barber, Tampa, FL

"Great book! This will help any entrepreneurial spirit begin the journey to starting and managing a business. The business tips will help business owners keep more of the profits and pay less in taxes. This is one of the best small business books I have ever read." LETTI UNDERHILL, Digicor, copierprinter.com, Tampa, FL

"This book has taught me so many things about business. The content is extremely informative and well written. The book concisely outlines the process of choosing the right business, raising capital for, and launching your new enterprise. I have taken away so much from this read and look forward to growing my marketing business." - KRISTIN FOLCH The Folch Group, thefolchgroup@gmail.com, Wesley Chapel, FL

Also, be sure to check out Ed Klaameyer's FREE eBook "The Savings Bible: 110 Savings Secrets You Can't Live Without"!

A free eBook download:

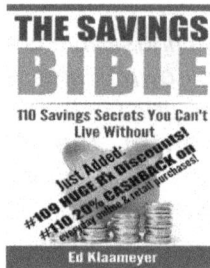

http://TheSavingsBibleBook.com

Send this free link to your family, friends and co-workers so they can begin to enjoy 110 savings secrets today! They will love you for it! Who do you know that likes to save money?

Ed is the founder of Global Profit Resources, LLC. This is a company dedicated to helping the small business person and entrepreneur (risk taker) to dominate their market specialty. If you want to become a strategic business entrepreneur and you own or manage a for-profit or not-for-profit business, Global Profit Resources, LLC is a difference maker. Check it out today: www.GlobalProfitResources.com

Creating Today's Entrepreneurs

www.ingramcontent.com/pod-product-compliance
Lightning Source LLC
Chambersburg PA
CBHW062019200326
41519CB00017B/4854